AF430530

Published by Traci Champion
ISBN 979-8-218-27829-8 (Paperback)
ISBN 979-8-218-27738-3 (Hardcover)

Ollie finds Christmas

By The Champion Family

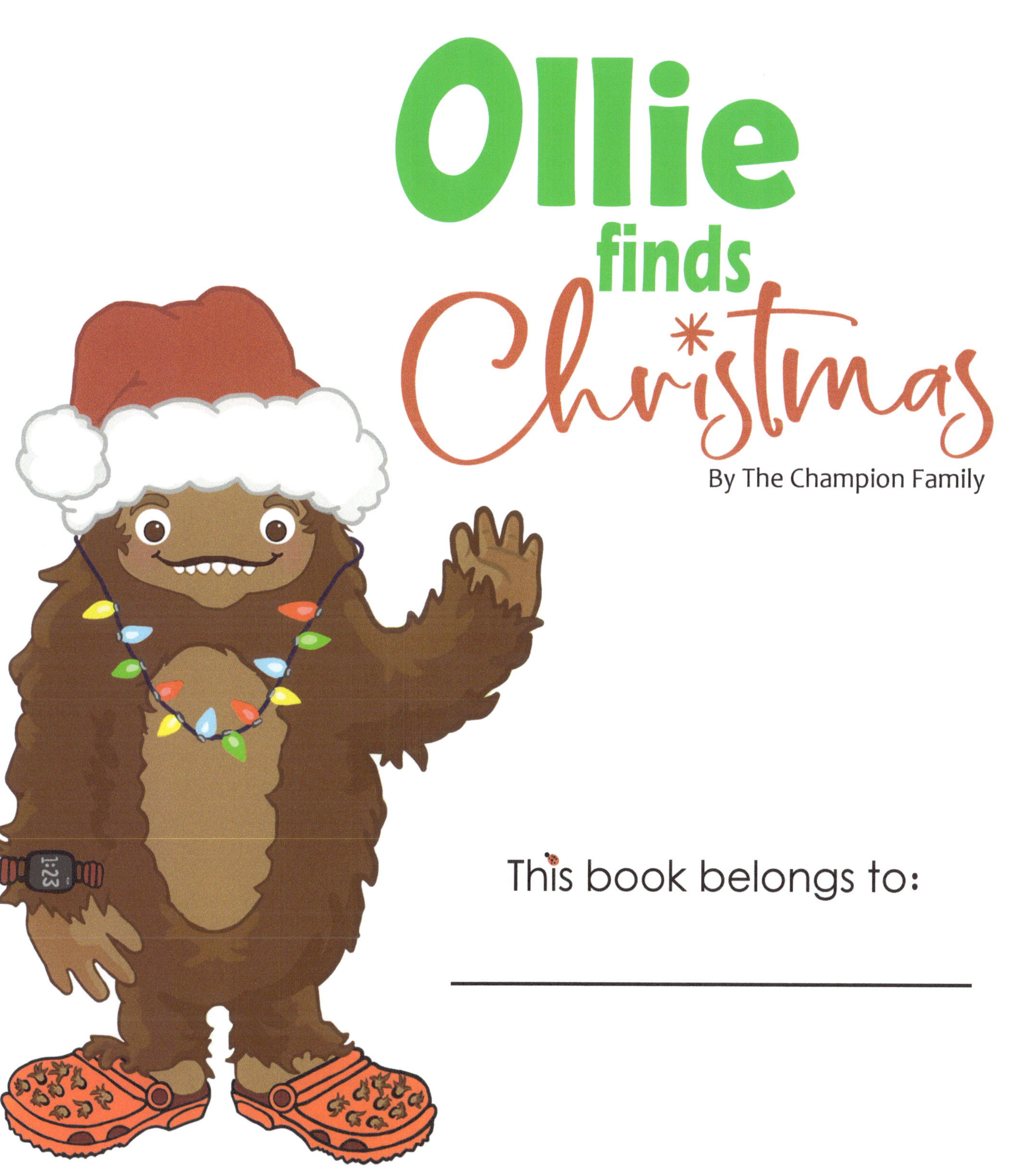

This book belongs to:

____

When the snow starts to fall
and the lights are all aglow.

It's easy to get caught up in
all the festive show.

But lets take a moment,
let's all recall.

The true meaning of
Christmas,
the greatest gift of all.

It's the most wonderful time
of the year.

Snowflakes fall, spreading
holiday cheer.

Building snowmen for all to
see.

Gathering with family and friends
around the tree.

We gather 'round with loved
ones near,

feeling love and spreading
holiday cheer.

But amidst the joy and laughter,
there is something more.

A feeling deep down inside that
we just can't ignore.

We decorate the tree with
colors so bright.

Ornaments of red, green,
and blue, what a wonderful
site.

The twinkling lights
illuminate the night sky,

as we sing carols and let
our spirits fly high.

Mia
ZoE
Max

It's not about the presents or the
twinkling lights.

It's not about the parties or the
cozy winter nights.

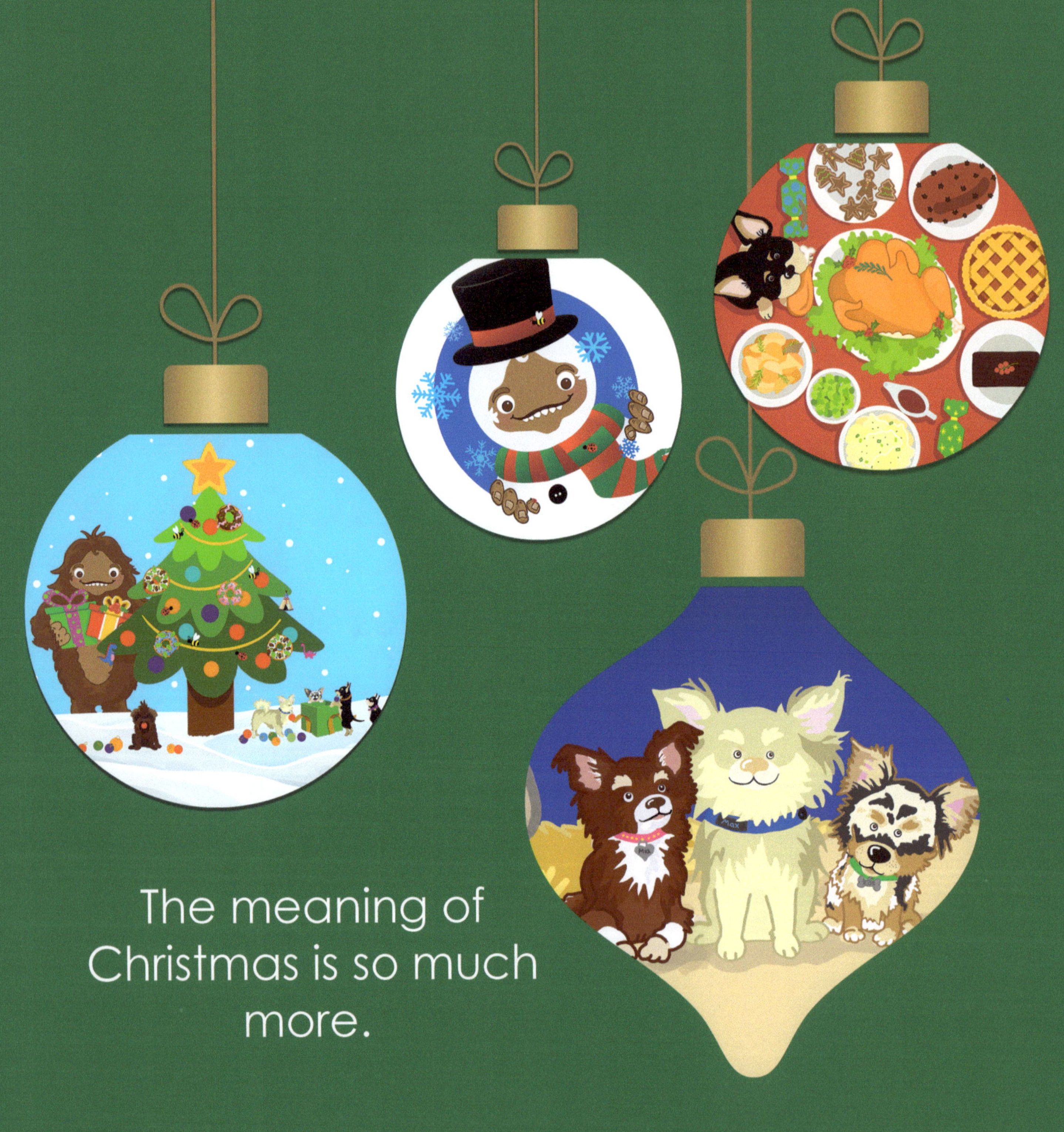

The meaning of
Christmas is so much
more.

A feeling
that makes our hearts
begin to soar.

The real meaning of Christmas
its so much more.

Baby Jesus' birthday, let our
hearts adore.

In a humble manger on that
holy night,

a baby was born bathed in
heavenly light.

He brought hope and joy,
a love that knows no end.

Baby Jesus, our Savior,
our forever friend.

So, as we celebrate this magical
season.

Let's remember Baby Jesus and
His reason.

His love and grace that fills us
with delight,

Merry Christmas to all and may
your hearts shine bright!

9 798218 278298